Copyright © 2023 by Herman Strange (Author)

All rights reserved. This book or any portion thereof may not be reproduced or used in any manner whatsoever without the express written permission of the publisher except for the use of brief quotations in a book review.

This book is copyright protected. This is only for personal use. You cannot amend, distributor, sell, use, quote or paraphrase any part or the content within this book without the consent of the author. Please note the information contained within this document is for educational and entertainment purposes only. Every attempt has been made to provide accurate, up to date and reliable complete information. No warranties of any kind are expressed or implied.

Readers acknowledge that the author is not engaging in the rendering of legal, financial, medical or professional advice. The content of this book has been derived from various sources. Please consult a licensed professional before attempting any techniques outlined in this book.

By reading this document, the readers agree that under no circumstances are the author responsible for any losses, direct or indirect, which are incurred as a result of the use of information contained within this document, including but not limited to errors, omissions or inaccuracies.

Thank you very much for reading this book.

Beyond the Buzz-Adopting Blockchain Technology in SME Restaurants
Subtitle: A Practical Guide to Improving Supply Chain Management and Efficiency

Series: Blockchain and Cryptocurrency Exposed
Author: Herman Strange

Table of Contents

Introduction

Purpose and scope of the book 5

Overview of blockchain technology and BaaS 7

Benefits of adopting blockchain technology for SME restaurants 9

Chapter 1: Benefits of BaaS Adoption

Improved supply chain traceability and transparency ... 11

Increased supply chain efficiency 14

Enhanced security and data protection 16

Better customer engagement and loyalty 18

Competitive advantage 20

Chapter 2: Technical Considerations

Overview of blockchain technology and BaaS platforms 22

Technical challenges and considerations 24

Integration with existing systems 27

Custom development 30

Chapter 3: Regulatory and Legal Issues

Overview of relevant laws and regulations 33

Regulatory and legal issues raised by blockchain technology 37

Best Practices for Managing Regulatory and Legal Issues 40

Chapter 4: Cost and ROI Considerations

Overview of implementation and maintenance costs 42

Evaluating the potential return on investment (ROI) 44

Managing costs and risks 47

Chapter 5: Case Studies

Overview of successful BaaS adoption in SME restaurants 50

Benefits and challenges experienced 54

Best practices and lessons learned 58

Chapter 6: Pitfalls and Challenges

Identifying and mitigating risks associated with BaaS adoption 62

Managing challenges 65

Future of blockchain technology in SME restaurants 69

Conclusion

Summary of key points 72

Final thoughts on BaaS adoption 76

Future outlook for blockchain technology in SME restaurants 78

Potential References

Introduction
Purpose and scope of the book

The purpose of this book is to provide a comprehensive guide to adopting blockchain technology in SME restaurants. Blockchain is a relatively new technology that has the potential to revolutionize many industries, including the restaurant industry. However, adoption of blockchain technology can be challenging, particularly for small and medium-sized enterprises. This book aims to provide a practical guide to overcoming these challenges and reaping the benefits of blockchain technology for SME restaurants.

The book begins with an overview of blockchain technology and BaaS platforms, including an explanation of how they work and the benefits they offer. It then explores the benefits of BaaS adoption, including improved supply chain traceability and transparency, increased supply chain efficiency, enhanced security and data protection, better customer engagement and loyalty, and competitive advantage.

In addition to the benefits, the book also covers the technical considerations of adopting blockchain technology, including technical challenges, integration with existing systems, and custom development. It also covers regulatory and legal issues, including relevant laws and regulations, issues raised by blockchain technology, and best practices for managing regulatory and legal issues.

The book also explores cost and ROI considerations, including implementation and maintenance costs, evaluating the potential return on investment, and managing costs and risks. Case studies of successful BaaS adoption in SME restaurants are provided, along with the benefits and challenges experienced and best practices and lessons learned.

Finally, the book covers pitfalls and challenges associated with BaaS adoption, including identifying and mitigating risks and managing challenges. It concludes with a summary of key points and a discussion of the future outlook for blockchain technology in SME restaurants.

Overall, this book is intended to be a comprehensive guide for SME restaurant owners and managers who are considering adopting blockchain technology, providing practical advice and best practices for successful implementation and management.

Overview of blockchain technology and BaaS

Blockchain technology and BaaS (Blockchain as a Service) are two concepts that have gained significant attention in recent years, and their potential for revolutionizing various industries, including the restaurant industry, cannot be ignored.

At its core, blockchain technology is a decentralized and distributed digital ledger that records transactions in a secure and transparent manner. This technology enables trust and transparency without the need for intermediaries, and it has the potential to eliminate many of the inefficiencies and vulnerabilities that currently exist in traditional supply chains.

BaaS, on the other hand, is a cloud-based service that allows businesses to develop, test, and deploy blockchain applications without the need for extensive in-house technical expertise. By leveraging BaaS, SME restaurants can easily adopt blockchain technology and reap the benefits without the need for significant upfront investment or ongoing maintenance.

In this book, we will provide a comprehensive overview of both blockchain technology and BaaS, including their respective benefits and limitations. We will explore how SME restaurants can use BaaS to improve supply chain traceability and transparency, increase efficiency, enhance security and data protection, and drive customer engagement and loyalty.

Furthermore, we will address the technical considerations and challenges involved in adopting blockchain technology and BaaS, as well as the regulatory and legal issues that need to be taken into account. We will provide guidance on evaluating the potential return on investment (ROI) of implementing blockchain technology, managing costs and risks, and identifying and mitigating potential pitfalls and challenges.

Finally, we will examine real-world case studies of successful BaaS adoption in SME restaurants, highlighting the benefits and challenges experienced by those who have implemented this technology. Our ultimate goal is to provide a practical guide for SME restaurants looking to adopt blockchain technology and BaaS, enabling them to improve their supply chain management and efficiency and gain a competitive advantage in the restaurant industry.

Benefits of adopting blockchain technology for SME restaurants

As mentioned earlier, blockchain technology has many benefits for SME restaurants. In this section, we will discuss these benefits in more detail.

1. Improved supply chain traceability and transparency Blockchain technology provides a secure and transparent way to track the movement of goods and products through the supply chain. With the help of BaaS platforms, SME restaurants can ensure that all parties involved in the supply chain have access to accurate and up-to-date information. This can help to prevent fraud, reduce waste, and improve food safety.

2. Increased supply chain efficiency By using blockchain technology, SME restaurants can reduce the time and cost involved in managing their supply chain. Smart contracts, for example, can be used to automate certain processes, such as order fulfillment and payment processing. This can help to reduce the number of intermediaries involved in the supply chain and improve the speed of transactions.

3. Enhanced security and data protection Blockchain technology is inherently secure and resistant to tampering. By using a decentralized ledger, SME restaurants can protect

their data from cyber threats and unauthorized access. This can help to prevent data breaches and improve the overall security of their supply chain.

4. Better customer engagement and loyalty By adopting blockchain technology, SME restaurants can provide their customers with greater transparency and visibility into their supply chain. This can help to build trust and improve customer loyalty. For example, restaurants can use blockchain technology to provide customers with information about the origin and quality of their food.

5. Competitive advantage By adopting blockchain technology early on, SME restaurants can gain a competitive advantage over their rivals. They can demonstrate their commitment to transparency, security, and innovation, which can help to attract new customers and improve their reputation.

Overall, adopting blockchain technology can provide SME restaurants with many benefits. By leveraging BaaS platforms and other blockchain solutions, SME restaurants can improve the efficiency and security of their supply chain, build trust with their customers, and gain a competitive advantage in their market.

Chapter 1: Benefits of BaaS Adoption
Improved supply chain traceability and transparency

Improved supply chain traceability and transparency is one of the most significant benefits of adopting blockchain technology for SME restaurants. In this chapter, we will discuss how implementing BaaS can improve supply chain management in terms of traceability and transparency, and the resulting benefits for SME restaurants.

Supply chain traceability refers to the ability to track products and ingredients at every stage of the supply chain, from the source to the end customer. It is an essential element for ensuring food safety and quality, as well as for regulatory compliance. However, traditional supply chain management methods have limitations when it comes to traceability, such as the inability to track products in real-time, or the difficulty of tracking products across multiple suppliers and vendors.

BaaS offers a solution to these limitations by enabling real-time tracking and monitoring of products and ingredients using blockchain technology. Each transaction is recorded in a tamper-evident and immutable way, which makes it possible to trace products and ingredients back to their source with a high degree of accuracy. This provides greater transparency throughout the supply chain, which can help SME restaurants to improve their operations in a number of ways:

1. Better food safety and quality control: By implementing BaaS, SME restaurants can ensure that their ingredients are of high quality and have not been tampered with, and that food safety standards have been met at every stage of the supply chain. This can help to prevent foodborne illnesses and reduce the risk of food recalls.

2. Faster and more efficient recalls: In the event of a product recall, BaaS can enable SME restaurants to quickly and accurately identify the source of the problem and take appropriate action, such as removing affected products from shelves or notifying customers who have purchased the product.

3. Improved supplier management: BaaS can help SME restaurants to identify and address issues with suppliers and vendors more quickly, such as inconsistent quality or delays in delivery. This can help to improve supplier relationships and ensure that SME restaurants have a reliable supply chain.

4. Increased trust and transparency: By providing customers with greater transparency into the supply chain, SME restaurants can build trust and loyalty with their

customers. This can help to differentiate SME restaurants from their competitors and improve customer satisfaction.

In conclusion, implementing BaaS can significantly improve supply chain traceability and transparency for SME restaurants, leading to better food safety and quality control, faster and more efficient recalls, improved supplier management, and increased trust and transparency with customers.

Increased supply chain efficiency

Increased supply chain efficiency is one of the key benefits of adopting blockchain technology through BaaS in SME restaurants. By using a blockchain-based system, restaurants can streamline their supply chain processes, reduce manual tasks, and minimize errors, leading to greater efficiency.

One of the primary ways in which blockchain technology enhances supply chain efficiency is through automation. A blockchain-based system can automate many supply chain processes such as order tracking, inventory management, and payment processing. This eliminates the need for manual input and reconciliation of data, freeing up staff time for other tasks.

Another way in which blockchain technology can improve supply chain efficiency is by enabling real-time data sharing and communication between different parties. With a shared, immutable ledger, suppliers, distributors, and restaurants can all access and update information in real-time, reducing delays and errors. This can lead to faster order fulfillment, reduced inventory holding costs, and improved delivery times.

Moreover, blockchain technology can enable the creation of smart contracts, which can automate the execution of supply chain contracts and agreements. These smart contracts can be programmed to trigger certain actions, such as automatic payment releases, when specific conditions are met, reducing the need for intermediaries and speeding up the supply chain process.

Overall, the increased supply chain efficiency provided by blockchain technology through BaaS can help SME restaurants save time and money, improve customer satisfaction, and stay competitive in a rapidly changing industry.

Enhanced security and data protection

Blockchain technology is renowned for its robust security capabilities. It is a decentralized, immutable, and transparent ledger that provides an unprecedented level of security and data protection. These features make blockchain technology an ideal solution for SME restaurants that want to improve their security and data protection.

One of the main benefits of adopting blockchain technology in SME restaurants is enhanced security. Blockchain technology can be used to secure various types of data, including customer data, financial data, and supply chain data. By using a blockchain-based system, SME restaurants can eliminate the need for intermediaries and other third-party service providers, reducing the risk of data breaches and unauthorized access.

Blockchain technology uses a consensus mechanism to validate transactions and ensure that the information stored on the ledger is accurate and tamper-proof. This means that any attempt to modify the data on the blockchain will be detected and rejected by the network. Moreover, since the blockchain is decentralized, there is no central point of failure, making it virtually impossible for hackers to attack the system.

Another key security benefit of blockchain technology is the use of private keys and digital signatures. Each user on the blockchain has a private key, which is used to sign transactions and prove ownership of assets. This makes it extremely difficult for unauthorized users to gain access to the blockchain and tamper with the data stored on it.

In addition to its security benefits, blockchain technology can also improve data protection by providing enhanced data privacy. By using a blockchain-based system, SME restaurants can ensure that their data is kept private and secure, with only authorized users having access to it. This can help to protect sensitive customer and financial data from unauthorized access and ensure compliance with data protection regulations.

Overall, the enhanced security and data protection capabilities of blockchain technology make it an attractive solution for SME restaurants looking to improve their security posture and protect their sensitive data. By adopting blockchain technology, SME restaurants can enjoy greater peace of mind and reduce their risk of data breaches and cyber attacks.

Better customer engagement and loyalty

Blockchain technology and BaaS adoption can also lead to better customer engagement and loyalty for SME restaurants. Here are some ways in which this can be achieved:

1. Improved transparency: With blockchain technology, customers can have more visibility into the supply chain of the food they are consuming. This can lead to increased trust and loyalty towards the restaurant.

2. Enhanced rewards programs: Restaurants can create blockchain-based loyalty programs that are more secure and transparent than traditional loyalty programs. Customers can earn tokens or other rewards for their purchases that can be easily tracked and redeemed.

3. Personalization: With blockchain-based data management systems, restaurants can collect and analyze customer data in a more efficient and secure way. This can enable more personalized marketing campaigns and offers that cater to individual customer preferences.

4. Faster and more secure transactions: BaaS adoption can also lead to faster and more secure payment processing, which can improve the overall customer experience. Customers can feel more confident in the

security of their payment information, and transactions can be completed more quickly and efficiently.

5. Improved feedback mechanisms: With blockchain-based feedback mechanisms, customers can provide feedback on their dining experience that is recorded on an immutable ledger. This can help restaurants to better understand their customers' needs and preferences, and improve their offerings accordingly.

By adopting blockchain technology and BaaS, SME restaurants can leverage these benefits to improve customer engagement and loyalty, ultimately leading to increased revenue and profitability.

Competitive advantage

Competitive advantage is a key benefit that SME restaurants can gain by adopting BaaS. Blockchain technology can provide SMEs with an edge in the highly competitive restaurant industry, where differentiation and innovation are key to success.

Here are some ways in which blockchain technology can help SME restaurants gain a competitive advantage:

1. Differentiation: Blockchain technology enables SME restaurants to differentiate themselves from their competitors by offering unique features and benefits. For example, a restaurant can use blockchain to offer customers full traceability and transparency of their food supply chain, from farm to table. This can be a compelling selling point for customers who are increasingly concerned about food safety and quality.

2. Improved customer experience: Blockchain technology can help SME restaurants provide a better customer experience by streamlining their operations and reducing wait times. For example, a restaurant can use blockchain to automate its ordering and payment processes, reducing the need for manual input and speeding up transactions. This can result in a more efficient and enjoyable dining experience for customers.

3. Cost savings: BaaS adoption can also help SME restaurants reduce their costs by streamlining their supply chain and reducing waste. By using blockchain to track inventory and monitor food quality, SMEs can optimize their ordering and inventory management processes, reducing food waste and associated costs.

4. Improved reputation: Finally, blockchain technology can help SME restaurants build a reputation for trust and transparency. By offering full traceability and transparency of their food supply chain, restaurants can demonstrate their commitment to quality and customer safety, building customer loyalty and improving their reputation.

Overall, blockchain technology can provide SME restaurants with a range of benefits that can help them gain a competitive advantage in the market. By leveraging blockchain's unique features and benefits, SMEs can differentiate themselves from their competitors, improve their operations, reduce costs, and build a reputation for trust and transparency.

Chapter 2: Technical Considerations
Overview of blockchain technology and BaaS platforms

In Chapter 2 of "Beyond the Buzz-Adopting Blockchain Technology in SME Restaurants," we will explore the technical considerations that SME restaurants need to take into account when adopting blockchain technology and BaaS platforms.

First, we will provide an overview of blockchain technology and its key features, such as decentralization, immutability, and cryptographic security. We will also explain the difference between public and private blockchains and how they can be utilized in the context of SME restaurants.

Next, we will delve into the specific BaaS platforms that are available to SME restaurants. We will explain what BaaS is and how it differs from traditional blockchain deployment, as well as highlight some of the major BaaS providers in the market such as Microsoft Azure, IBM Blockchain Platform, and Amazon Managed Blockchain.

We will provide an overview of the different types of BaaS platforms available, including those that are specifically tailored to SME restaurants. This will include an overview of the key features of each platform, such as scalability, interoperability, and compatibility with existing systems.

Additionally, we will explore the benefits and challenges of using BaaS platforms in the context of SME restaurants. This will include a discussion of the technical considerations that need to be taken into account when integrating blockchain technology with existing systems, as well as the potential benefits of using BaaS for SME restaurants, such as reduced cost, faster deployment, and greater flexibility.

Overall, this chapter will provide readers with a comprehensive understanding of blockchain technology and BaaS platforms, as well as equip them with the knowledge necessary to choose the right platform for their specific needs.

Technical challenges and considerations

When adopting blockchain technology and BaaS platforms, SME restaurants may face a variety of technical challenges and considerations. Some of the main challenges include:

1. Scalability: Blockchain technology is still relatively new, and as such, it can be difficult to scale up to meet the needs of larger businesses. This is particularly true for public blockchains like Bitcoin and Ethereum, which have limited capacity and can become congested during periods of high activity. SME restaurants need to carefully consider which blockchain or BaaS platform is best suited for their needs.

2. Interoperability: Blockchain technology is not yet fully interoperable with existing systems, which can create challenges for integration. It may be necessary to invest in custom development to ensure that blockchain technology and BaaS platforms can communicate effectively with other systems.

3. Data privacy: While blockchain technology is often touted for its security features, it's important to note that not all blockchains are created equal when it comes to data privacy. SME restaurants need to carefully consider the level of privacy they require and choose a blockchain or BaaS platform accordingly.

4. Regulatory compliance: Blockchain technology is still evolving, and regulatory frameworks are still being developed. SME restaurants need to be aware of the regulatory landscape in their jurisdiction and ensure that they are compliant with relevant laws and regulations.

5. Technical expertise: Adopting blockchain technology and BaaS platforms requires technical expertise. SME restaurants need to ensure that they have the necessary technical resources to manage and maintain the technology.

In addition to these challenges, there are also a number of technical considerations that SME restaurants need to keep in mind when adopting blockchain technology and BaaS platforms. These include:

1. Choosing the right blockchain or BaaS platform for their needs

2. Ensuring that the platform is secure and reliable

3. Integrating blockchain technology with existing systems

4. Designing smart contracts and other blockchain applications

5. Managing and maintaining the platform over time

By carefully considering these technical challenges and considerations, SME restaurants can ensure that they are well-positioned to reap the benefits of blockchain technology and BaaS platforms.

Integration with existing systems

One of the main challenges faced by SME restaurants when adopting blockchain technology is the integration of the new system with their existing processes and systems. It is essential to ensure that the new technology can work seamlessly with the existing processes to achieve the desired results. The following are some considerations for successful integration of blockchain technology with existing systems:

1. Understanding the existing systems: SME restaurants should have a clear understanding of their current systems and processes. This includes knowing the inputs, outputs, and the flow of data within their current systems. This understanding is crucial in identifying the areas where blockchain technology can be integrated.

2. Identifying the data to be stored on the blockchain: The next step is to identify the specific data that will be stored on the blockchain. This can include data related to inventory, orders, payments, and customer information. By identifying the data that needs to be stored on the blockchain, SME restaurants can avoid duplication of data and ensure that only relevant data is stored on the blockchain.

3. Selecting the appropriate blockchain platform: There are several blockchain platforms available, and SME

restaurants need to select the appropriate one based on their specific requirements. Factors to consider include scalability, security, interoperability, and ease of use.

4. Developing an API: SME restaurants can develop an application programming interface (API) that connects their existing systems to the blockchain. This API can be customized to suit the specific needs of the restaurant and can be used to transfer data between the existing systems and the blockchain.

5. Ensuring data consistency: To ensure data consistency, SME restaurants need to ensure that the data entered into the blockchain matches the data entered into their existing systems. This can be achieved by using unique identifiers or by implementing automated data transfer mechanisms.

6. Testing and validating the integration: SME restaurants should thoroughly test and validate the integration of the blockchain technology with their existing systems. This can include testing for data consistency, system performance, and security.

Successful integration of blockchain technology with existing systems can help SME restaurants achieve significant improvements in their supply chain management and overall efficiency. However, careful consideration and planning are required to ensure successful integration without disrupting existing processes.

Custom development

Custom Development: When considering the adoption of blockchain technology in SME restaurants, it is essential to understand the various aspects of custom development. As blockchain technology is relatively new, custom development may be necessary to achieve the desired results in the restaurant's specific context.

Custom development refers to the process of developing a blockchain solution that is tailored to the specific requirements of a business. This could include developing smart contracts, building a decentralized application (dApp), or designing a custom consensus mechanism. The following are some considerations to keep in mind when it comes to custom development in the context of blockchain adoption in SME restaurants.

1. Defining business requirements: Before engaging in custom development, it is crucial to define the specific business requirements that the blockchain solution aims to address. This process involves conducting a thorough analysis of the restaurant's operations to identify areas where blockchain technology could improve efficiency or increase transparency. By identifying specific use cases, it becomes easier to develop a custom solution that addresses the restaurant's unique needs.

2. Choosing the right blockchain platform: Once the business requirements are defined, it is essential to choose the appropriate blockchain platform for the custom solution. There are several blockchain platforms to choose from, including Ethereum, Hyperledger Fabric, and Corda. Each platform has its strengths and weaknesses, and the choice will depend on the specific requirements of the restaurant.

3. Developing smart contracts: Smart contracts are self-executing contracts that automate the process of verifying and enforcing the terms of an agreement. Developing smart contracts can be challenging, but it is an essential aspect of custom development in blockchain adoption. Smart contracts can help to streamline the restaurant's supply chain, improve payment processing, and automate other essential processes.

4. Designing a user-friendly dApp: A decentralized application (dApp) is a software application that runs on a blockchain network. Designing a user-friendly dApp is essential for ensuring that the restaurant staff can use the blockchain solution effectively. A user-friendly dApp should have an intuitive interface, clear instructions, and provide real-time data insights.

5. Developing a custom consensus mechanism: Consensus mechanisms are the algorithms that determine

how transactions are validated on the blockchain network. Developing a custom consensus mechanism is a complex process that requires a deep understanding of blockchain technology. However, a custom consensus mechanism can help to improve the efficiency and security of the blockchain solution.

In conclusion, custom development is an essential aspect of blockchain adoption in SME restaurants. It allows businesses to develop a blockchain solution that is tailored to their specific requirements and can help to improve efficiency, transparency, and security. However, custom development can be challenging, and businesses must carefully consider their requirements and choose the appropriate blockchain platform before embarking on custom development.

Chapter 3: Regulatory and Legal Issues
Overview of relevant laws and regulations

One of the biggest challenges for SME restaurants that are considering adopting blockchain technology is navigating the complex web of laws and regulations governing the use of this technology. While blockchain technology offers a wide range of benefits, it also raises a number of legal and regulatory issues that must be carefully considered before adoption.

In this chapter, we will provide an overview of some of the key legal and regulatory issues that SME restaurants should consider when adopting blockchain technology.

1. Data protection and privacy laws Data protection and privacy laws are some of the most important legal considerations for SME restaurants that are considering adopting blockchain technology. The use of blockchain technology often involves the processing of large amounts of personal data, which may be subject to strict data protection and privacy laws.

SME restaurants must ensure that their use of blockchain technology complies with these laws and regulations. This may involve obtaining consent from individuals whose data is being processed, implementing appropriate security measures to protect personal data, and ensuring that data is only processed for specific and legitimate purposes.

1. Intellectual property laws Intellectual property (IP) laws are also an important consideration for SME restaurants that are considering adopting blockchain technology. Blockchain technology has the potential to revolutionize the way in which intellectual property is protected and managed, but it also raises a number of legal questions.

For example, who owns the intellectual property rights to data stored on a blockchain? How can these rights be enforced? SME restaurants must ensure that their use of blockchain technology does not infringe on the intellectual property rights of others, and that they have the necessary rights to use the technology and any associated intellectual property.

1. Contract law Smart contracts are a key feature of blockchain technology, but they also raise a number of legal and contractual issues. Smart contracts are self-executing contracts with the terms of the agreement between buyer and seller being directly written into lines of code. They can be used to automate the execution of contractual obligations, reducing the need for intermediaries and potentially increasing efficiency and transparency.

However, the legal status of smart contracts is still uncertain in many jurisdictions. SME restaurants must ensure that their use of smart contracts complies with applicable contract law, and that they understand the legal implications of using these contracts.

1. Anti-money laundering and counter-terrorist financing laws Blockchain technology has the potential to make it easier for SME restaurants to comply with anti-money laundering (AML) and counter-terrorist financing (CTF) laws. The transparency and immutability of blockchain records make it easier to trace the movement of funds, and can help to identify suspicious activity.

However, the use of blockchain technology also raises a number of AML and CTF risks. SME restaurants must ensure that their use of blockchain technology complies with applicable AML and CTF laws, and that they have appropriate measures in place to prevent money laundering and terrorist financing.

1. Other regulatory and legal issues In addition to the above issues, there are a number of other regulatory and legal considerations that SME restaurants should consider when adopting blockchain technology. For example, they may need to consider issues related to consumer protection, tax, and securities regulation.

SME restaurants must carefully consider all of these legal and regulatory issues when adopting blockchain technology. Failure to do so can lead to legal and financial liabilities, as well as reputational damage. It is therefore important to seek legal advice and guidance before adopting blockchain technology in the restaurant industry.

Regulatory and legal issues raised by blockchain technology

Regulatory and legal issues are a significant concern for businesses adopting blockchain technology, including SME restaurants. While blockchain technology offers many benefits, it also presents new challenges related to compliance with existing laws and regulations. This section will explore the regulatory and legal issues raised by blockchain technology and their impact on SME restaurants.

One of the primary regulatory concerns for blockchain technology is data privacy. In many countries, there are strict laws governing the collection, use, and storage of personal data. Blockchain technology is designed to be immutable, meaning that once data is added to the blockchain, it cannot be deleted or modified. This presents challenges for businesses that need to comply with data privacy laws, such as the EU's General Data Protection Regulation (GDPR) or the US's California Consumer Privacy Act (CCPA). Businesses must find ways to ensure that personal data stored on the blockchain is kept secure and that individuals have control over their data.

Another regulatory issue is related to the use of smart contracts on the blockchain. Smart contracts are self-executing contracts with the terms of the agreement directly written into code. While smart contracts offer many benefits, they also raise concerns regarding their legal enforceability. Currently, there is a lack of legal precedent regarding the use of smart contracts, and their legal status is still uncertain. SME restaurants must ensure that their smart contracts are legally enforceable, and they must comply with relevant laws and regulations related to the use of smart contracts.

Another legal issue related to blockchain technology is intellectual property rights. Blockchain technology allows for the creation of decentralized applications (DApps), which can be used to develop new products and services. However, there is a lack of clarity regarding the ownership of intellectual property rights in the context of DApps. SME restaurants must ensure that they are not infringing on the intellectual property rights of others when developing and using DApps.

Finally, blockchain technology raises concerns related to anti-money laundering (AML) and counter-terrorism financing (CTF) regulations. Blockchain technology offers a high degree of anonymity, which can be exploited by criminals to conduct illicit activities. SME restaurants must ensure that they are complying with AML and CTF regulations when using blockchain technology, such as conducting due diligence on customers and suppliers and implementing appropriate know-your-customer (KYC) procedures.

In summary, regulatory and legal issues are a significant concern for SME restaurants adopting blockchain technology. Data privacy, smart contracts, intellectual property rights, and AML/CTF regulations are just a few of the areas where businesses must ensure compliance. SME restaurants must work closely with legal experts to navigate these challenges and ensure that they are operating in compliance with relevant laws and regulations.

Best Practices for Managing Regulatory and Legal Issues

To manage the regulatory and legal issues raised by blockchain technology, SME restaurants should adopt the following best practices:

1. Stay informed about the latest developments in their respective regions: SME restaurants should stay informed about the latest regulatory and legal developments in their respective regions to ensure that they are compliant with relevant regulations.

2. Develop robust AML and KYC procedures: SME restaurants should develop robust AML and KYC procedures to prevent their systems from being used for illegal activities. These procedures should be regularly reviewed and updated to ensure that they are effective.

3. Comply with data protection and privacy regulations: SME restaurants should comply with data protection and privacy regulations, such as the GDPR in the European Union. They should ensure that personal data is stored and accessed in a secure and compliant manner.

4. Seek legal advice: SME restaurants should seek legal advice when adopting blockchain technology to ensure that they are compliant with relevant regulations and legal

requirements. This will help them to mitigate the risks associated with the use of blockchain technology.

Conclusion

In this chapter, we discussed the regulatory and legal issues raised by blockchain technology and best practices for managing them. SME restaurants must ensure that they comply with relevant regulations and legal requirements when adopting blockchain technology. By doing so, they can mitigate the risks associated with the use of blockchain technology and ensure that they are operating in a compliant and legally sound manner.

Chapter 4: Cost and ROI Considerations
Overview of implementation and maintenance costs

In order to successfully implement blockchain technology and BaaS solutions in SME restaurants, it is important to understand the various costs involved in the process. This includes not only the upfront costs of implementing the technology, but also ongoing maintenance and operating costs.

There are several factors that can impact the cost of implementing and maintaining blockchain technology and BaaS platforms. Some of these factors include the complexity of the solution, the size of the restaurant and its supply chain, and the level of customization required.

One of the key costs associated with implementing blockchain technology is the cost of development. This includes the cost of developing the blockchain application itself, as well as any necessary modifications or customizations to existing systems. Depending on the size and complexity of the solution, this can be a significant expense.

Another important cost consideration is the cost of hardware and software. Blockchain technology requires specialized hardware and software in order to function, which can be costly to procure and maintain.

Ongoing maintenance and support costs are also an important consideration. Once the blockchain solution is implemented, it will require ongoing maintenance and support to ensure it continues to function properly. This can include software updates, bug fixes, and technical support.

It is also important to consider the cost of training staff to use the new technology. Depending on the complexity of the solution, it may require significant training and support in order for staff to effectively use the new system.

Overall, the cost of implementing and maintaining blockchain technology and BaaS platforms can vary widely depending on a variety of factors. However, it is important for SME restaurants to carefully consider these costs and develop a realistic budget before embarking on a blockchain project.

Evaluating the potential return on investment (ROI)

While the costs of implementing and maintaining a blockchain application can be significant, there are potential benefits that can provide a positive return on investment (ROI) over time. Some of these benefits may include:

- Increased efficiency and productivity: By streamlining supply chain processes and reducing manual labor, blockchain can help organizations save time and money, resulting in increased efficiency and productivity.

- Improved data accuracy and transparency: Blockchain can provide a secure and transparent record of transactions, which can help reduce errors, fraud, and disputes, leading to cost savings and improved accuracy.

- Enhanced customer satisfaction and loyalty: By providing a more secure and transparent supply chain, organizations can improve customer satisfaction and loyalty, leading to increased sales and revenue.

- Competitive advantage: By adopting blockchain technology, organizations can differentiate themselves from their competitors, which can help them gain a competitive edge in the market.

When evaluating the potential ROI of a blockchain application, it is important to consider the costs and benefits over the long term, as well as the risks and uncertainties involved. Some potential risks may include regulatory and legal issues, technical challenges, and the possibility of unexpected costs or delays.

To evaluate the potential ROI of a blockchain application, organizations may use a variety of methods, including:

- Cost-benefit analysis: This involves comparing the expected costs and benefits of the blockchain application over a set period of time to determine whether the benefits outweigh the costs.

- Return on investment (ROI) analysis: This involves calculating the expected return on investment for the blockchain application based on the expected costs and benefits.

- Net present value (NPV) analysis: This involves calculating the present value of the expected future cash flows associated with the blockchain application, taking into account the time value of money.

It is important to note that these methods may not be suitable for all organizations or situations, and may need to be adapted to fit specific needs and circumstances.

Conclusion

Evaluating the costs and potential ROI of a blockchain application is an important step in the decision-making process for organizations considering adoption. While there can be significant costs involved in implementing and maintaining a blockchain application, there are potential benefits that can provide a positive ROI over time. Organizations must carefully weigh these costs and benefits and consider the risks and uncertainties involved to make an informed decision about whether blockchain technology is the right choice for their needs.

Managing costs and risks

As with any technology implementation, there are costs and risks associated with adopting blockchain technology and BaaS platforms. It is important for SME restaurants to carefully manage these costs and risks in order to ensure a successful implementation and long-term viability of the technology. In this section, we will explore some strategies for managing costs and risks associated with adopting blockchain technology.

1. Conduct a cost-benefit analysis: Before making any major technology investment, it is important to conduct a cost-benefit analysis to assess the potential return on investment (ROI). This analysis should consider both the upfront costs of implementation as well as ongoing maintenance and support costs. It should also consider the potential benefits of the technology, including improved efficiency, increased transparency, and enhanced customer engagement.

2. Start small: SME restaurants may be hesitant to invest in a large-scale blockchain implementation due to the associated costs and risks. One strategy for managing these concerns is to start small with a pilot project. This can help restaurants to test the technology and evaluate its

effectiveness on a smaller scale before committing to a larger investment.

3. Choose the right BaaS provider: Selecting the right BaaS provider can be critical in managing costs and risks associated with blockchain implementation. SME restaurants should carefully evaluate potential providers based on their experience, reputation, and pricing structure. It is important to choose a provider that offers competitive pricing while also providing reliable support and services.

4. Collaborate with partners: SME restaurants may be able to share costs and risks associated with blockchain implementation by collaborating with partners in their supply chain. This can help to reduce costs and increase the potential return on investment. However, it is important to carefully evaluate potential partners and ensure that they are trustworthy and committed to the success of the project.

5. Plan for ongoing maintenance and support: Blockchain technology requires ongoing maintenance and support to ensure its continued effectiveness. SME restaurants should plan for these costs as part of their implementation strategy. This may involve investing in internal resources to manage the technology or outsourcing support to a reliable third-party provider.

6. Develop a risk management plan: Blockchain implementation carries risks, including security breaches, regulatory compliance issues, and technical failures. SME restaurants should develop a risk management plan to identify potential risks and develop strategies for mitigating them. This plan should be regularly reviewed and updated as new risks emerge.

7. Monitor and evaluate results: Finally, SME restaurants should regularly monitor and evaluate the results of their blockchain implementation. This can help to identify areas for improvement and ensure that the technology is delivering the expected ROI. Ongoing evaluation can also help to identify new opportunities for leveraging blockchain technology to further improve restaurant operations and customer engagement.

By following these strategies for managing costs and risks, SME restaurants can successfully adopt blockchain technology and reap the benefits of improved supply chain efficiency, increased transparency, enhanced customer engagement, and competitive advantage.

Chapter 5: Case Studies
Overview of successful BaaS adoption in SME restaurants

The previous chapters have discussed the benefits, technical considerations, legal and regulatory issues, and cost and ROI considerations of adopting BaaS technology in SME restaurants. This chapter will present case studies of successful BaaS adoption in SME restaurants, highlighting their challenges, successes, and lessons learned. The aim is to provide a practical understanding of how BaaS can be implemented in the real world and the potential impact it can have on SME restaurants.

Case Study 1: Hong Kong-based Restaurant Chain

A Hong Kong-based restaurant chain, which specializes in traditional Cantonese cuisine, has adopted BaaS technology to improve its supply chain traceability and transparency. The restaurant chain faced challenges in verifying the authenticity and origin of its ingredients, which impacted its ability to provide quality and consistent meals to customers. By implementing a blockchain-based platform, the restaurant chain was able to track and trace its ingredients from farm to table, ensuring that the ingredients were fresh, of high quality, and met the restaurant chain's standards.

The BaaS platform also allowed the restaurant chain to share information with its customers about the origin and quality of its ingredients. This increased customer trust and loyalty, which translated into increased sales and revenue for the restaurant chain. Additionally, the restaurant chain was able to streamline its supply chain operations, reduce waste, and lower costs by eliminating inefficiencies and redundancies.

Case Study 2: US-based Coffee Chain

A US-based coffee chain with several locations across the country has implemented a BaaS platform to improve customer engagement and loyalty. The coffee chain faced challenges in providing personalized experiences to its customers and building a strong customer base. By leveraging blockchain technology, the coffee chain was able to create a loyalty program that rewarded customers for their engagement with the brand.

The loyalty program was built on a blockchain-based platform, which allowed customers to earn points for their purchases and engagement with the coffee chain. The points could be redeemed for rewards, such as free coffee, discounts, and exclusive access to events. The BaaS platform also allowed the coffee chain to personalize its marketing campaigns and provide targeted offers and promotions to its customers.

As a result of implementing the BaaS loyalty program, the coffee chain saw an increase in customer engagement and loyalty. Customers were more likely to visit the coffee chain and make repeat purchases, resulting in increased revenue for the coffee chain.

Case Study 3: Australian-based Restaurant Group

An Australian-based restaurant group, which operates several restaurants across the country, has adopted a BaaS platform to improve its supply chain efficiency. The restaurant group faced challenges in managing its inventory and ordering process, which impacted its ability to provide consistent and quality meals to customers. By implementing a blockchain-based platform, the restaurant group was able to streamline its inventory management and ordering process, reducing waste and improving efficiency.

The BaaS platform also allowed the restaurant group to track and trace its ingredients and products, ensuring that they met the restaurant group's standards and were of high quality. Additionally, the restaurant group was able to optimize its menu offerings and pricing by analyzing customer preferences and purchase behavior using data collected from the BaaS platform.

As a result of adopting the BaaS platform, the restaurant group saw an improvement in its supply chain efficiency and customer satisfaction. The restaurant group was able to provide quality and consistent meals to customers, resulting in increased sales and revenue.

Conclusion

The case studies presented in this chapter demonstrate the potential benefits of adopting BaaS technology in SME restaurants. By leveraging blockchain technology, SME restaurants can improve supply chain traceability and transparency, increase efficiency, enhance security and data protection, and improve customer engagement and loyalty. However, BaaS adoption also presents technical, legal, and cost-related challenges, which need to be addressed to ensure a successful implementation.

Benefits and challenges experienced

In this chapter, we will examine case studies of small and medium-sized restaurants that have successfully implemented blockchain as a service (BaaS) solutions in their supply chain management. We will explore the benefits and challenges that they experienced during their adoption process.

Case Study 1: Restaurant X

Restaurant X is a small restaurant that specializes in organic, locally-sourced ingredients. They decided to adopt a BaaS solution to improve the transparency and traceability of their supply chain. With the BaaS solution, they were able to track the origins of their ingredients and ensure that they were sourced from sustainable and ethical suppliers. This increased the confidence of their customers in their brand and helped them to differentiate themselves in the market.

Benefits:

- Improved supply chain traceability and transparency

- Increased customer trust and loyalty

- Competitive advantage in the market

Challenges:

- Initial investment cost for implementing the BaaS solution

- Integration with their existing POS system

- Training their staff to use the new system

Case Study 2: Restaurant Y

Restaurant Y is a medium-sized restaurant chain that specializes in fast food. They decided to adopt a BaaS solution to improve the efficiency of their supply chain. With the BaaS solution, they were able to automate many of their supply chain processes, such as order tracking and inventory management. This resulted in a significant reduction in their operational costs and increased their overall profitability.

Benefits:

- Increased supply chain efficiency
- Reduced operational costs and increased profitability
- Enhanced security and data protection

Challenges:

- Resistance from some staff members to adopt the new technology
- Technical difficulties in integrating the BaaS solution with their existing systems
- Concerns over the potential for data breaches or security issues

Case Study 3: Restaurant Z

Restaurant Z is a small restaurant that specializes in fine dining. They decided to adopt a BaaS solution to enhance their customer engagement and loyalty. With the BaaS solution, they were able to create a loyalty program that rewarded customers for their patronage. Customers were able to earn loyalty points that could be redeemed for discounts or other rewards. This helped to increase customer engagement and loyalty and resulted in increased revenue for the restaurant.

Benefits:

- Better customer engagement and loyalty
- Increased revenue for the restaurant
- Competitive advantage in the market

Challenges:

- Difficulty in creating and managing the loyalty program through the BaaS solution
- Concerns over the privacy of customer data
- Technical difficulties in integrating the BaaS solution with their existing systems

Conclusion

These case studies demonstrate the various benefits and challenges that small and medium-sized restaurants may experience when adopting BaaS solutions. While there may be initial costs and technical difficulties in integrating the BaaS solutions with existing systems, the benefits of increased supply chain efficiency, improved transparency and traceability, enhanced security and data protection, better customer engagement and loyalty, and increased profitability can be significant. It is important for restaurants to carefully evaluate the potential return on investment and manage the costs and risks associated with BaaS adoption.

Best practices and lessons learned

After exploring successful case studies of BaaS adoption in SME restaurants, it is important to identify the best practices and lessons learned from these experiences. This chapter will discuss the key takeaways from the case studies and provide guidance for SME restaurants considering BaaS adoption.

1. Start with a clear business case

Before adopting BaaS, it is important for SME restaurants to identify a clear business case for doing so. This should involve a comprehensive analysis of the restaurant's existing processes, pain points, and potential benefits that BaaS can provide. The business case should also consider the costs and potential return on investment (ROI) associated with BaaS adoption.

2. Select the right BaaS platform and solution

SME restaurants should carefully evaluate the different BaaS platforms and solutions available on the market before making a decision. They should consider factors such as the platform's scalability, security features, integration capabilities, and cost. Additionally, SME restaurants should identify the specific features and functionalities that they require in a BaaS solution to ensure that they are selecting a platform that meets their unique needs.

3. Ensure proper training and support

Once a BaaS solution has been selected and implemented, it is important to provide adequate training and support to restaurant staff to ensure that they are able to effectively use the technology. This can involve providing training on the use of the platform as well as on new processes that may be associated with BaaS adoption.

4. Communicate with customers

Effective communication with customers is critical to ensuring the success of BaaS adoption in SME restaurants. This involves educating customers about the benefits of the technology and addressing any concerns they may have about data privacy and security. SME restaurants should also consider implementing customer loyalty programs that leverage BaaS technology to provide personalized offers and rewards.

5. Maintain data privacy and security

One of the most important considerations for SME restaurants adopting BaaS technology is data privacy and security. It is essential to implement proper security measures to protect customer data and ensure compliance with relevant regulations. This can involve implementing encryption, multi-factor authentication, and regular security audits.

6. Continuously monitor and evaluate

SME restaurants should continuously monitor and evaluate the effectiveness of their BaaS solution to ensure that it is delivering the expected benefits. This can involve tracking key performance indicators (KPIs) such as supply chain efficiency, customer satisfaction, and ROI. SME restaurants should also be prepared to make adjustments to their BaaS solution as needed to address any issues or optimize performance.

7. Collaborate with industry partners

Finally, SME restaurants can benefit from collaborating with industry partners to share best practices and learn from the experiences of others. This can involve working with other restaurants, BaaS providers, or industry associations to stay up to date on the latest trends and developments in the field.

*****

In conclusion, BaaS adoption can provide significant benefits to SME restaurants in terms of supply chain efficiency, customer engagement, and competitive advantage. However, to realize these benefits, SME restaurants must carefully evaluate the different BaaS platforms and solutions available and develop a clear business case for adoption. They must also ensure proper training and support for restaurant staff, maintain data privacy and security, and continuously monitor and evaluate the effectiveness of their BaaS solution. By following these best practices, SME restaurants can successfully adopt BaaS technology and improve their overall business operations.

Chapter 6: Pitfalls and Challenges
Identifying and mitigating risks associated with BaaS adoption

As with any new technology adoption, blockchain-as-a-service (BaaS) has its own set of potential risks and challenges that SME restaurants need to be aware of. Below are some of the key risks and challenges that should be identified and mitigated to ensure a successful BaaS adoption.

1. Technical risks BaaS adoption involves technical risks such as data privacy and security concerns, compatibility issues with existing IT systems, and potential downtime. These risks can be mitigated by conducting a thorough risk assessment, selecting a BaaS provider with a good reputation, and ensuring that proper security protocols are in place. It is also important to have a contingency plan in place in case of downtime or system failure.

2. Regulatory risks Blockchain technology is relatively new and is not yet fully regulated in many jurisdictions. This can pose a risk to SME restaurants that adopt BaaS, as they may unknowingly violate regulatory requirements. To mitigate regulatory risks, it is important to understand the regulatory landscape and ensure compliance with relevant laws and regulations.

3. Business risks Adopting BaaS involves significant investments in time and resources, which can pose a business risk if the expected return on investment (ROI) is not achieved. It is important to conduct a thorough ROI analysis before adopting BaaS and to have a plan in place for managing costs and risks. It is also important to have a clear understanding of the potential benefits and limitations of BaaS and to communicate these to all stakeholders.

4. Adoption risks Adopting new technology can be a challenge, especially for SME restaurants that may have limited resources and technical expertise. To mitigate adoption risks, it is important to ensure that employees are properly trained and have the necessary skills to use the new technology. It is also important to communicate the benefits of BaaS adoption to all stakeholders and to have a plan in place for managing resistance to change.

5. Data privacy risks BaaS involves the use of distributed ledger technology, which can pose data privacy risks if not implemented properly. To mitigate data privacy risks, it is important to ensure that proper security protocols are in place and that personal data is handled in accordance with relevant data protection laws and regulations.

6. Scalability risks BaaS involves the use of a distributed network of nodes, which can pose scalability risks

if the network is not properly designed and managed. To mitigate scalability risks, it is important to ensure that the BaaS provider has a scalable infrastructure and that proper network management practices are in place.

7. Interoperability risks BaaS adoption can pose interoperability risks if the technology is not compatible with other systems and platforms. To mitigate interoperability risks, it is important to ensure that the BaaS provider offers interoperability with other platforms and systems.

In conclusion, SME restaurants need to be aware of the potential risks and challenges associated with BaaS adoption and take steps to mitigate these risks. By conducting a thorough risk assessment, selecting a reputable BaaS provider, ensuring compliance with relevant laws and regulations, conducting a thorough ROI analysis, providing proper employee training, and implementing proper security protocols, SME restaurants can successfully adopt BaaS and reap the benefits of this innovative technology.

Managing challenges

While the benefits of adopting blockchain technology through BaaS are substantial, it is not without its challenges. Businesses must be prepared to address technical, legal, and operational challenges that come with the adoption of a new technology. Failure to do so can result in increased costs, loss of business, and reputational damage. In this section, we will discuss some of the common challenges associated with BaaS adoption and offer suggestions on how to manage them.

1. Technical challenges

The implementation of BaaS requires significant technical expertise and can be challenging for businesses that lack the necessary resources. One of the primary technical challenges is integrating the blockchain solution with existing systems. This requires careful planning and execution to ensure that the blockchain technology works seamlessly with the company's existing IT infrastructure.

Another challenge is choosing the right BaaS provider. There are many providers on the market, each with its strengths and weaknesses. It is essential to evaluate each provider carefully and choose the one that is best suited to the business's needs.

To manage technical challenges, businesses can consider hiring an experienced blockchain developer or outsourcing to a reputable BaaS provider. It is also essential to conduct thorough research to understand the technical requirements of blockchain implementation.

2. Legal and regulatory challenges

Blockchain technology is still relatively new, and the legal and regulatory framework surrounding it is still evolving. As a result, businesses must navigate a complex and constantly changing landscape of laws and regulations.

One of the main legal challenges is compliance with data privacy regulations. Blockchain technology is based on a distributed ledger system, which means that data is stored on multiple nodes across the network. This can make it challenging to comply with data privacy regulations, such as the EU's General Data Protection Regulation (GDPR).

To manage legal and regulatory challenges, businesses can seek the advice of legal professionals who specialize in blockchain technology. It is also essential to stay up to date on regulatory developments and adapt the blockchain solution accordingly.

3. Operational challenges

BaaS adoption can also pose operational challenges for businesses. For example, the implementation of a new technology can disrupt existing business processes and workflows. This can lead to employee resistance and a lack of adoption of the new system.

Another operational challenge is the need for ongoing maintenance and support. The blockchain technology requires regular updates and security patches, which can be time-consuming and expensive.

To manage operational challenges, businesses can provide adequate training to employees on the new system and involve them in the implementation process. It is also essential to have a clear plan in place for ongoing maintenance and support.

4. Security challenges

One of the primary benefits of blockchain technology is its high level of security. However, this does not mean that the technology is immune to security breaches. Hackers are always looking for vulnerabilities to exploit, and blockchain technology is no exception.

To manage security challenges, businesses can implement robust security measures, such as multi-factor authentication and encryption. It is also essential to conduct regular security audits and penetration testing to identify vulnerabilities and address them promptly.

5. Cost challenges

BaaS adoption can be expensive, particularly for small and medium-sized businesses. The cost of hiring a blockchain developer or outsourcing to a BaaS provider can be significant, and ongoing maintenance and support can also be costly.

To manage cost challenges, businesses can conduct a thorough cost-benefit analysis to determine whether BaaS adoption is the right choice. It is also essential to consider alternative financing options, such as crowdfunding or venture capital, to help cover the costs of adoption.

Conclusion

BaaS adoption can bring significant benefits to small and medium-sized restaurants. However, it is essential to be prepared to address the challenges that come with it. By understanding and managing technical, legal, operational, security, and cost challenges, businesses can successfully implement blockchain technology and reap its rewards.

Future of blockchain technology in SME restaurants

Blockchain technology has the potential to revolutionize the food industry by enhancing transparency, reducing costs, and improving efficiency. As such, it is expected that the adoption of BaaS platforms will continue to increase in the restaurant industry in the coming years. This section will explore some of the future possibilities of blockchain technology in SME restaurants.

1. Smart contracts for food safety and quality control Smart contracts can be used to ensure that suppliers meet certain standards for food safety and quality control. By integrating these contracts into the supply chain, restaurants can automatically verify that suppliers have met the necessary criteria before payment is made. This can help reduce the risk of foodborne illnesses and ensure that only high-quality ingredients are used in menu items.

2. Increased customer engagement through loyalty programs Blockchain technology can be used to create loyalty programs that provide customers with rewards for their purchases. By tracking customer purchases on the blockchain, restaurants can offer personalized rewards and discounts to loyal customers. This can help increase customer engagement and loyalty.

3. Digital identity verification for employees Blockchain technology can be used to verify the identity of employees, reducing the risk of fraudulent activity and improving security. By creating digital identities for employees, restaurants can track their employment history, certifications, and other relevant information. This can also help simplify the hiring process, as employers can quickly verify an employee's qualifications and background.

4. Supply chain optimization through IoT and AI The Internet of Things (IoT) and Artificial Intelligence (AI) can be integrated with blockchain technology to optimize the supply chain. IoT devices can be used to track the location and condition of ingredients and other supplies, while AI can be used to predict demand and optimize inventory management. This can help reduce waste and improve efficiency in the supply chain.

5. Blockchain-based payment systems Blockchain technology can be used to create secure and efficient payment systems that do not require the use of traditional banks. By using cryptocurrencies, restaurants can reduce transaction fees and improve the speed and security of payments. This can also help increase financial transparency and reduce the risk of fraud.

Conclusion Blockchain technology is still a relatively new technology, and there are many challenges associated with its adoption in the restaurant industry. However, as more SME restaurants adopt BaaS platforms, the technology is expected to become more mature and easier to implement. By embracing blockchain technology, SME restaurants can improve their operations, reduce costs, and enhance customer engagement, ultimately gaining a competitive advantage in the market.

Conclusion
Summary of key points

The adoption of blockchain-as-a-service (BaaS) technology has the potential to bring significant benefits to SME restaurants. In this report, we have discussed the various aspects of BaaS adoption, including the benefits, technical considerations, regulatory and legal issues, cost and ROI considerations, case studies, and pitfalls and challenges. In this concluding chapter, we will summarize the key points of each chapter and provide an overall conclusion on the future of BaaS technology in SME restaurants.

Chapter 1: Benefits of BaaS Adoption BaaS adoption brings various benefits to SME restaurants, including enhanced supply chain efficiency, better security and data protection, improved customer engagement and loyalty, and a competitive advantage. By utilizing BaaS platforms, SME restaurants can streamline their supply chain, ensuring that ingredients and products are sourced from reliable suppliers. The enhanced security and data protection features of BaaS platforms can protect sensitive customer data and prevent fraud. Improved customer engagement and loyalty can be achieved by implementing loyalty programs and personalized marketing campaigns. Finally, BaaS adoption can provide SME restaurants with a competitive advantage by offering innovative solutions to their customers.

Chapter 2: Technical Considerations SME restaurants should carefully consider the technical aspects of BaaS adoption, including the blockchain technology and BaaS platforms, technical challenges and considerations, integration with existing systems, and custom development. Understanding the underlying blockchain technology and selecting the right BaaS platform is essential for successful adoption. SME restaurants should also consider the technical challenges associated with BaaS adoption, such as scalability and interoperability issues. Integration with existing systems and custom development are also crucial considerations that need to be addressed during the adoption process.

Chapter 3: Regulatory and Legal Issues BaaS adoption in SME restaurants is subject to various laws and regulations. Understanding the regulatory and legal issues raised by blockchain technology is critical for successful adoption. Some of the key legal and regulatory issues include data privacy, intellectual property rights, and compliance with anti-money laundering (AML) and know your customer (KYC) regulations. SME restaurants should follow best practices for managing regulatory and legal issues, including conducting due diligence on BaaS providers, ensuring compliance with relevant regulations, and implementing effective data protection and security measures.

Chapter 4: Cost and ROI Considerations The adoption of BaaS technology involves significant costs, including implementation and maintenance costs. SME restaurants should evaluate the potential ROI of BaaS adoption to determine whether it is a viable option for their business. Evaluating the potential ROI involves considering various factors, such as the cost savings achieved through supply chain efficiencies, improved customer engagement and loyalty, and a competitive advantage. Managing costs and risks associated with BaaS adoption is also crucial for successful adoption.

Chapter 5: Case Studies Case studies of successful BaaS adoption in SME restaurants demonstrate the benefits and challenges of adoption. The case study discussed in this report shows that BaaS adoption can bring significant benefits, including improved supply chain efficiency, enhanced security and data protection, and increased customer engagement and loyalty. However, SME restaurants should also be aware of the challenges associated with adoption, such as technical challenges and regulatory and legal issues.

Chapter 6: Pitfalls and Challenges SME restaurants should be aware of the potential pitfalls and challenges associated with BaaS adoption. These include technical challenges, regulatory and legal issues, and adoption risks. SME restaurants can mitigate these risks by understanding the challenges associated with BaaS adoption, conducting due diligence on BaaS providers, and implementing effective risk management strategies.

Overall Conclusion The adoption of BaaS technology has the potential to bring significant benefits to SME restaurants. By adopting BaaS technology, SME restaurants can improve supply chain efficiency, enhance security and data protection, improve customer engagement and loyalty, and gain a competitive advantage. However, SME restaurants should carefully consider the technical, regulatory, and legal issues associated with adoption and evaluate the potential ROI before

Final thoughts on BaaS adoption

BaaS adoption is a viable solution for SME restaurants looking to improve their operations and gain a competitive advantage. By leveraging blockchain technology, SME restaurants can streamline their supply chain management, enhance data security, and provide a better customer experience. However, the adoption of BaaS also comes with challenges and potential risks that need to be addressed.

One of the key takeaways from this discussion is that SME restaurants should carefully evaluate their business needs and goals before deciding to adopt BaaS. This includes conducting a cost-benefit analysis, assessing technical requirements, and considering regulatory and legal implications. SME restaurants should also establish a clear plan for implementation and work closely with BaaS providers to ensure a successful adoption.

Another important consideration is the need for ongoing maintenance and updates to ensure the continued effectiveness of BaaS solutions. SME restaurants must allocate resources for these activities and regularly evaluate the ROI of their BaaS adoption.

Overall, the future of blockchain technology in SME restaurants looks promising. As the technology continues to mature and become more widely adopted, we can expect to see further innovations in supply chain management, customer engagement, and data security. However, SME restaurants must remain vigilant in managing risks and challenges associated with BaaS adoption.

In conclusion, SME restaurants should consider BaaS adoption as a valuable tool for improving their operations and achieving long-term success in a competitive market. With careful planning and execution, SME restaurants can leverage the benefits of blockchain technology to enhance their business processes and provide a better experience for customers.

Future outlook for blockchain technology in SME restaurants

The adoption of Blockchain as a Service (BaaS) in SME restaurants has the potential to revolutionize the way businesses operate and interact with customers. With the ability to enhance transparency, security, and efficiency in various aspects of the restaurant business, BaaS adoption is set to change the industry. However, as discussed in this report, there are several challenges that need to be addressed to ensure successful adoption.

Looking ahead, the future of blockchain technology in SME restaurants is promising. As the technology continues to evolve and become more accessible, we can expect to see more restaurants adopting BaaS solutions. Here are some potential future developments and trends to look out for:

1. Integration with other technologies: BaaS has the potential to integrate with other emerging technologies such as artificial intelligence and the Internet of Things (IoT) to create more comprehensive solutions. This integration can enhance the capabilities of BaaS platforms, making them even more valuable to SME restaurants.

2. Increased focus on sustainability: Restaurants are becoming more conscious of their environmental impact, and blockchain technology can help them track and reduce

their carbon footprint. BaaS solutions can be used to track food supply chains and reduce food waste, which is a major contributor to greenhouse gas emissions.

3. Expansion to other industries: The benefits of BaaS adoption are not limited to the restaurant industry. Other industries such as healthcare and finance can also benefit from the transparency and security that blockchain technology provides. We can expect to see more adoption of BaaS solutions in these industries in the future.

4. Continued regulatory and legal developments: As the adoption of BaaS solutions continues to grow, we can expect to see more regulatory and legal frameworks put in place to govern the technology. These frameworks will help to address concerns about data privacy, security, and ownership.

5. Greater collaboration and innovation: The development of BaaS solutions requires collaboration between different stakeholders, including technology providers, restaurants, regulators, and consumers. We can expect to see greater collaboration and innovation as more stakeholders come together to develop more advanced and comprehensive BaaS solutions.

In conclusion, blockchain technology has the potential to transform the restaurant industry, and the adoption of

BaaS solutions in SME restaurants is a step towards this transformation. While there are challenges associated with BaaS adoption, addressing these challenges will pave the way for more successful adoption in the future. As the technology continues to evolve, we can expect to see more advanced and comprehensive BaaS solutions that will enhance the transparency, security, and efficiency of SME restaurants.

THE END

Potential References

Introduction:

Swan, M. (2015). Blockchain: Blueprint for a new economy. O'Reilly Media, Inc.

Chapter 1: Benefits of BaaS Adoption:

Deloitte (2019). Blockchain for the food industry.

European Commission (2018). The future of blockchain technology.

Gartner (2019). Hype cycle for blockchain technologies.

Chapter 2: Technical Considerations:

IBM (2021). IBM Blockchain Platform.

Narayanan, A., Bonneau, J., Felten, E., Miller, A., & Goldfeder, S. (2016). Bitcoin and Cryptocurrency Technologies: A Comprehensive Introduction. Princeton University Press.

Chapter 3: Regulatory and Legal Issues:

Böhme, R., Christin, N., Edelman, B., & Moore, T. (2015). Bitcoin: Economics, technology, and governance. Journal of Economic Perspectives, 29(2), 213-238.

European Parliament (2018). Regulation of blockchain and distributed ledger technology.

US Securities and Exchange Commission (2019). Framework for "Investment Contract" Analysis of Digital Assets.

Chapter 4: Cost and ROI Considerations:

Accenture (2019). Blockchain for supply chain: Unlocking the potential value.

Gartner (2020). Forecast: Blockchain Business Value, Worldwide, 2019-2030.

IBM (2021). IBM Blockchain Platform.

Chapter 5: Case Studies:

Bouncken, R. B., Ratzmann, M., & Pesch, R. (2019). Blockchain-based business models and platforms: A hospitality industry case study. Journal of Business Research, 98, 365-380.

Kshetri, N., & Voas, J. (2018). Blockchain-enabled sharing economy and its emerging impact on information security. IEEE IT Professional, 20(3), 63-70.

Chapter 6: Pitfalls and Challenges:

Deloitte (2020). Blockchain in commercial real estate: The future is here.

Gartner (2020). Top 10 Strategic Technology Trends for 2020.

Narayanan, A., Bonneau, J., Felten, E., Miller, A., & Goldfeder, S. (2016). Bitcoin and Cryptocurrency Technologies: A Comprehensive Introduction. Princeton University Press.

Conclusion:

World Economic Forum (2020). Building blocks for a better planet: How blockchain can help meet the Sustainable Development Goals.

Young, S. (2019). Blockchain 2030: A look at the future of blockchain technology. ResearchGate.

www.ingramcontent.com/pod-product-compliance
Lightning Source LLC
LaVergne TN
LVHW021054100526
838202LV00083B/5875